THROW YOURSELF INTO THE PRAIRIE

Throw Yourself into the Prairie

POEMS

Francesca Chabrier

Sarabande Books

LOUISVILLE, KENTUCKY

FIRST EDITION

Managing Editor
Sarabande Books, Inc.
2234 Dundee Road, Suite 200
Louisville, KY 40205

Library of Congress Cataloging-in-Publication Data

Chabrier, Francesca, 1983–
[Poems. Selections]
Throw yourself into the prairie : poems / Francesca Chabrier.—First edition.
    pages cm
Includes bibliographical references and index.
ISBN 978-1-936747-65-8 (pbk. : alk. paper)
I. Title.
PS3603.H28T57 2014
811'.6—dc23

                        2013011706

Cover image by Emily Hunt.
Cover and text design by Kirkby Gann Tittle.

Manufactured in Canada.

This book is printed on acid-free paper.

Sarabande Books is a nonprofit literary organization.

The Kentucky Arts Council, the state arts agency, supports Sarabande Books with state tax dollars and federal funding from the National Endowment for the Arts.

02 14

for my friends and my family

CONTENTS

PROLOGUE

PEACH SOME LAID THEIR HANDS ON

Peach some laid their hands on and they fell off.
An afternoon meal of peaches.
A cloud does not dapple the sky: they are in touch
the peach in the heat
and the slow-moving hands.
A litter of peaches squished
and one peeling itself in the shade.
I am who loves it here.
I eat a peach with my whole mouth
and can see everything.
Peach is French for a feeling
like be still be exactly still.

CHAPTER ONE

THE POPULAR TREE

There is a popular tree
that lives year round.
Maybe it will live forever
who knows
there is no one
that can touch it.
People come
from all around
to see the popular tree.
It holds a nest
made out of gloves.
I should say that the tree
is not gigantic. It is
about as big as a man
of average size
without a head
or shoulders.
The tree is
so incredible that
when I walk up to it,
my legs shake.
I want to lick
the leaves of the tree.
I want to watch it
get struck by lightening
and turn to neon.
This is not because

I want to destroy the tree.
It's because sometimes
it is fun to watch things
misbehave.

CHEEK AGAINST SOFT PUMPKIN FUR

I am me, but I am a cow.
You are a river.
You think I am cute.
You call me kitten-cow.
You are a river, but your water
looks like a hologram
and when I look at you,
I see a fake reflection.
You tell me I am wearing
five scarves even though
I have mittens on.
I throw a coin at you,
but you are not a fountain.
You ask me to meow
for you, but I won't.
I feed you chocolate, and we play that game
where I write on your leg with my finger.
You brush my hair for 2 hours
while I spell things like:
cheek against soft pumpkin fur, and
I would come to you on a rubber gull.
The eyes and the faces become less easy
to make out in the night,
but we go on and on.
Wax ponyfish. Japanese fog.
I am stupid at stopping.

THE WHITE MACHINE

The white machine is packed with lights.
The machine is white
because it has let the snow collect.
There is a baby inside
the machine. There are stars,
and also a deep place you can go
to see Machu Picchu.
The machine
produces white paper. The paper
is smooth like the voice I am using
to talk to you. I write a letter
on the paper and slide it under your door.
Hello, please give me back
the umbrella you borrowed.
When rain falls on the machine,
it bubbles first and then produces a noise
that sounds like passing through
an aisle of shaking trees.
This is the sound of the machine crying.
The machine is white
and eats white bread. White milk.
The machine runs on white milk. It
collects snow. It holds the baby.
I smack the machine and the baby shakes.
Inside there are mummies wrapped in white paper.
A telephone rings.
Hello, I will not give you back your umbrella.

The snow turns to rain and makes white puddles.
The baby swims in the water,
and floats on the surface like a bottle.
The white machine is tired. I hold it
and kiss it with my clean white hands.

A PLACE FOR EVERYTHING

All morning, I walk around with a bag over my head.
My mother calls on the telephone. She wears a paper hat. She
keeps it in her pocketbook while she is sleeping. "I want to join
in," I tell her. I fold the bag into a sombrero. Outside, there
are no ships. The bay is foggy and still. I am exhausted. I am
like a runner about to cross the finish line at the end of a very
important race. When you ask me to love you, I rise up like a
balloon. I ring your doorbell five times. I wait for you to have
me in and hang up my hat.

THE WORLD HAS TURNED AND LEFT ME HERE

You are getting a root canal
at a dentist's office in Waco.
You do not live in Waco,
and you are still sleepy
from flying. When the stewardess
asked everyone to turn off
their electronic devices, they did,
but you left your walkman on.
The plane was descending
through the part of the sky
where you are in the clouds completely.
A woman was floating.
She was wearing wings
made out of tin foil.
You tapped on the window and said
are you god and she said yes I am god,
and she turned into a sharp edged silver ball.
The ball dropped down faster than the plane,
you felt so overcome
you ripped out your teeth.
When you arrived in Waco
there was a sign that said
Home of the Largest Tin Foil Ball.
There was a parade you stayed to watch
your favorite band pass by on a float.
You were in pain, you threw your tooth
at the lead singer, he used it as a pick.

SEPTEMBER

September is fooling me.
I am wearing an enormous sweater.
I am looking for wool socks in the shape
of California, the word for footprint,
green green hills in a shoebox diorama.

There is no pattern to my behavior.
In her head, my mother calls me outrageous.
On the telephone this morning she called me
quixotic, and I imagined her
imagining me, holding a chandelier
that looks like an octopus who has just swallowed
a very large number of votive candles.

Dear whoever you are,
without you, the streets feel wet
and missing. I am no good
at weather systems, and my head
is soaked and lazy. Tonight
the aquarium looks boring and unlit.
Inside, there is a walrus rustling.
He is not dreaming.
He is merely tossing in his sleep.

Immediately after lunch I will write you
a letter telling you I drew your face
and hung it on my wall. Good morning you,
I say. In my best cursive I will also tell you
that at night I love when I turn over
and you are not moving; a potato.
Sometimes it is so cold I want to freak out.
You blow hot into my ear.
My face is drowning. Your hands are a net.

CHAPTER TWO

THE END OF THE LONESOME ERA

The internet means I want to touch you.
I write to you on the internet to say hello,
why don't you try and touch me too.
I found a lettuce growing machine on the internet.
I found tiny cans of oatmeal, and a replica
of a painting that I printed out and hung on my wall.
The internet feels like almost being someplace.
It feels like doing a pretty normal thing
somewhere strange, like playing fetch in a graveyard.
Behind a veil of clean glass, there are so many eyes.
I thought mine were hazel, but it said they are brown.
The internet never sleeps. It is millions of spiders.
Big spiders and little spiders. Spiders whose bodies feel like linen.
Spiders that look fierce. Spiders that are harmless.
Spiders that move in the dark and behave like the sea.

GERARD

you knew better
and I was wrong,
but you keep coming back
to say it.
I am the white heat,
not of earth, but shiny
like a sequin,
bright lights in winter.
I'm standing on the wistful ledge
of living a hard life.
You come toward me
and I move
like a silver energy inside you.
Thank you for the good
and patient attitude.
It bloomed into an eye.
Time is heavy
and pressing like a winter coat.
Just think, it is really me
piling the snow
to cover your house.
I am a woman who does things
for no good reason and I accept this.

COFFEE MAKES PEOPLE SMART

It's really cold here
and silver today
tiny flecks
of snow everywhere

I love you Yoko Ono

I am 1-20 of hundreds
and there is no one on my mind

I am in my house clothes
drinking from a jar
playing out a dream bbq in my head

it's a combination
of last night's fire and the i-ching

fra angelico

the sky is as open as a blouse
and you'll be a woman soon

my dear
fra angelico you wretched thing

why don't you take some coffee
and in the bathroom
in the morning please
clear your throat

INSTRUCTIONS ON HOW TO

Instructions on how to write a novel:

Begin with the following passage: *Mimilo was born in the war. A premature orphan left next to a white stone in a prairie. Tiny by all standards, with not a bit of hair and eyes the size of planets; green and round.* Change Mimilo's name. Be sure she never finds out who her mother is. She will marry a sentinel. Scatter her ashes in the river Seine.

Instructions on how to imitate an angel:

Eat rice until it feels like there is a pillow in your stomach. Designate enough time and space in your day to be sure it remains fluffed.

Instructions on how to anticipate crossword puzzle answers:

Shakespeare's food of love, Gasket type, Numerical prefix, Little swab.

Instructions on espionage:

Draw what is happening outside your window with your non-dominate hand. Now close your eyes and draw what you imagine happening inside your neighbor's house with your dominant hand.

Instructions on how to get married:

Build a box from weathered wood. Fill it with melon. Do not freeze, dry or boil the fruit. Nail the flaps of the box to its body, and wait one full calendar year before opening it. Inside there will be a pink jewel. Pass it on.

Instructions on how to fight loneliness:

When you are home alone, make a meal by following a recipe, but without preparing a tidy mise en place. Say out loud what you are doing (everything) as you are doing it (the whole time). Do not stop talking.

Instructions on how to hibernate for winter:

Enter a TV-darkened room. Realize that there are problems that seem very serious, but they will not exist once the snow melts. The woman in the movie that is being broadcast is breathtakingly beautiful. If the telephone rings, unplug it.

Instructions on how to build a net:

()—()—()—()—()—()
()—()—()—()—()—()
()—()—()—()—()—()
()—()—()—()—()—()

Instructions on how to prepare for a ritual of longing:

PART 1:

Write non-stop for 15 minutes in front of a fire. Throw the paper into the fire. Do not think too hard about loss.

PART 2:

Learn to let go of your lover if his ship has passed. Accept that something is missing. Fill it with water.

BAD NIGHT, GOOD MORNING

I was born
in February
a little fish
for my mother
Happy Birthday
wrapped in ribbon
I love you
so much
I only have
so much
time on this earth
is a mindfuck
and people
are impossible
to understand
but I am not trying
the sun is shining
and spilling
all over the place
like me
falling in love
feels like a job
but that's over
I am standing
and singing
this morning
I was thinking

it's probably nice
to be a fish
but I am happy
to have legs
and I am wearing new socks

WHEN I LOOK UP AND SEE / I AM WALKING

hello memory
hello simple me
happening again in a new
ordinary day
hello sister,
and rain, truth
written on the wall.
Hello exceptions,
slap on the wrist.
oh hello, goodbye.
I ask you sweetly
for every piece of me
would go back to tip
something else over.
Hello spongy hope in a glass,
dried up and sorry,
orchestrated so poorly.
Say hello
to my mother and father.
I am sorry
I cannot be with them.
Hello out there
in the distance.
I know I came here
for this
simple me
a man's man,
I am just learning

my way around.
Hello red light in the shower
secret and silent
in the new house.
Take me back
to before I was born
so I can say hello
again for the first time.

CHAPTER THREE

THE BEAUTIFUL POEM

Beautiful Australian girls wearing pinafores under the umbrellas of Business Executives in the rain

Beautiful Antarctic girls riding on the backs of dorados, holding fish heads in their cold, dusty, curving arms

Beautiful Hawaiian girls swimming in circles

Beautiful girls from Shangri-la, all Capricorns, all left-handed, chartering helicopters to the Memphis skyline

Beautiful Taino girls giving birth to babies that sleep in glass cradles

Beautiful Swiss girls climbing Mont Blanc in Phys. Ed.

Beautiful Lithuanian girls with blonde hair and golden thighs pencil diving into the Baltic Sea

Beautiful Irish girls playing house on an island otherwise entirely populated by subversive politicians

Beautiful Antiguan girls playing cricket near Galley Bay

Beautiful Earth girls are easy

Beautiful Irish girl, you are crunked in a totally green dress, you are paranormal, you have a headlamp in the grass, you are digging and can see China

Beautiful Korean girls snapping pictures of the dam

Beautiful fed-up, hard-up, knocked-up, locked-up, stuffed-up, worked-up, beat-up girls

Beautiful girls from Brixton who admire all that is gilded and excessive, with a passion for luxury, and a love of Oriental clothes

Beautiful Fijian girls drinking high-quality, reserved, silver needle tea

Beautiful Italian girls working in a factory near Siena that produces mahogany torture racks with platinum chains

Beautiful girls from Zanzibar walking across raffia beams holding handfuls of counterfeit cash

Natural Disasters and then: dancehalls with natural lighting, where natural beauties with natural haircolor & natural instincts play Russian Roulette

Beautiful Spanish girls of Moorish descent, longing to hear music, active in the pursuit thereof, digging for musettes in arenas

Beautiful Romanian girls stretching before breakfast, mounting a single, chalky beam, dismounting perfectly into their coach's arms

Beautiful girls on experimental diets flying without cargo on a biplane over the coast of Normandy

Beautiful Arab girls sewing puppets of djinns

Beautiful Argentinean girls with clear skin, glossy hair, sound teeth, bright eyes & experience fornicating in all British overseas territories

Beautiful American girls, completely unmagnificent, holding themselves together by the ends of their braids

CHAPTER FOUR

★

Elizabeth, don't cry.
I love you friends.
Inside this tiny vessel
there is a Viking.
He is kicking and asking me to marry him.

LOW

There was a room
and we were
two people in it.
You were the most
difficult thing
in the room.
When you screamed
it went black and became
a little bit smaller.
I put my face
against your ear
and could hear the wind.
There was also the sun.
Then July
and a woman.
We were just breathing
there inside the room.
This heart of mine
you kept saying.
We put on our swimsuits
in the dark.
There was a pool,
but no pool light.
No way to make
buffalo shadows
with our hands.
There were curtains.
They were aquamarine.

The floor was flat,
but began moving.
First you were eaten
by the dark.
I was alone
and eating the curtains.

I WILL BREAK THE SILENCE IN
HOLLAND APPALOOSA

Today I am here inside a tone-deaf cabin
I am here I have traveled by bus
There are some things I don't like to talk about
I would rather hold you and sing
a cowboy song your heart all thumping in Dutch
I am a real woman with long braids
I am expert in detecting subterranean spunk
You will feel yourself stunned the banjo
I am singing I am not getting the words right
What I want to say is my darling
I am the yellow flower amongst the totally blue fields,
but what you hear is honey take my coat and cover up
because it's raining like hell and pounding like hooves.

AN ANNOUNCEMENT

I mean this to enter
a conversation
to call out to you :
hello I am here
a living thing
and you,
beauty, finished,
in the frost.
Dividing, I scream to you,
I lift my voice
in the old room
folding a blanket,
having trouble lifting
the heavy luggage and no one
will meet me
to unlock the buckle
while boarding the plane
under 6 hours of thunder.
I couldn't help myself
but pay attention
to the floating, bickering,
to stay up late is to push
through toward the green
sun like a lamp in a field.
I got so mad wandering
up to the lightening,
love twisting a pinched
ribbon piling up all over my face.

I shake off other people,
tape over the lesser part
of a hole in the wall, your
whole life on the film
of my somber memory
and I cannot carry on
the river, fully drifting out.

I WILL SEE YOU OUTSIDE / A LITTLE HEAP

Things are going okay
I saw kids running

Your head was leaking
& I operated by tearing

away at the first layer
So little was exposed

you handed me a tool
to get the right feeling

There is no floor
I have no canoe

This afternoon in reverse
is a moviehouse all full of wind

I can't help but wonder
Where is the big eye

& what a difference a day
does not always make

POEM FOR PITTSBURGH

I was walking over after I scribbled on an umbrella
and I said I've worked too little
for weeks but that is the best I could come to.
You understood, and lifted the umbrella
to show me why you had stopped breathing.
Then I took my hands out of the kitchen sink and thought
about the time I gave up to leave and
went to Pittsburgh. I was positive that everyone
I knew was going to Pittsburgh, but I couldn't help them
because I was the one making them
into Pittsburgh. It is what I hoped to be the result. I got
married. I gave you a new kitchen sink.
I spread Pittsburgh all over my wedding dress.
You were hung over, so I sewed a pocket on your face.
I keep going on pretending I am sure
about what I am doing, but I am only beginning to know
about Pittsburgh because it's easy.
Before we keep disappearing we grow
larger. The kitchen sink is just a way to say you
have become bony and weary from the rain.
I ask you to press your cheek against my wedding dress.
It is a ritual I would like to put behind.
I was walking over before dinner. I'd had too much wine.
Pittsburgh set fire in me, I was teeming, and my love. . . .

CHAPTER FIVE

THE AXIOMS

You are a very grey number 2.
You cracked yourself in half
and found a silver 2
to make you feel whole again.
You only want to be 2
like a missing twin
searching deep into a forest
to find that 1 underneath
the only flower.
You are my father grey number 2.
You are not able to stand
straight in the wind.
You are so strange
you bony number.
In the forest we beat dead animals
1 by 1
until we can get their hearts
to go in line with our own.
It feels so right to be a number 2,
to hang yourself out on a line
in the rain for 1 whole year
so you can turn to silverish.
And then your sister,
you have only 1 sister,
will polish you to look like her.
When 2 splits it is like 1 right ear
and a very small ledge.
It is also like a swan on dry land.

Today I found 1 quarter on a shelf,
but left it there for someone else.
Child, you must save so you can build
things that will grow beautiful.
The need I have for you
is gone, and father now I am
in 1 brand new forest.
It is a green and darkening room.
At night I pitch a tent and sleep
with my clothes on. I am sorry
I am just one grey fool.

3 is a natural number.
It is a green dress
on a beautiful woman
with enormous breasts.
I feel safe with the idea
of your arms around me,
but I cannot actually touch you,
so I take 3 steps back.
When there is an appetite for more,
we buy 2 and get 1 free.
3 is a fullback in the rain.
It is the soft and sleepy middle,
and what turns a coincidence
into that's just the way things go.
There is you and me
and another one.
We sleep in pyramid shaped rooms
so we can converge.
3 is an ear lobe.
It is the way I whisper
lottery numbers
to the demented bronze statue.
I am 1 of 3 sisters and we have
commissioned a family portrait.
The photographer says, on the count of 3,
but she is nodding off
while her tripod drops into the lake.

9 you are a fugitive.
You are a tiny embryo
and therefore perishable.
There is good news and
then there is bad news.
Try even living once.
I am sick with it.
9 is so many chances.
It is like stalling a nerve
in a bright and casual hospital.
I am not frightened of you,
but you are tricky.
You can cast the dizziest spell with 6.
And then there are all of the planets
you keep to yourself.
Look at you!
With the moon perched on your neck
as if it were your actual head.
In the daylight I can see you
are trying to wave the hole
of a bagel on an incredibly bent pole.
But you are just a gnarly ribbon.
You are an interstate
where all of the cars in the world
come to a standstill.
You are unforgivable,
but I can see you
are also alone.

I advise that you be rational
and position yourself on a cloud.
This way when there is a lasso,
because there always is a lasso,
you will be prepared.

11 is 2 bodies and these 2 bodies
want to crash into each other,
but there is no ambulance.
It is a nook of totem poles
on a stubby road and also
2 modest giraffes peering
at something unruly in the grass.

7 is this rainbow.
And we go to walk beneath it,
but there is no throughway,
only a room with a fat sky.
And there are animals in there.
For example, there are bears
and a man in there.
The man is you.
An orchestra is playing
while opera singers pretend
to know many arias, and somehow
they are getting it right in there.
There is a round of applause,
and the conductor is taking a modest bow
by craning his neck just so.
A lamppost is giving off
a wicked and ominous glow in there.
We are rolling
dice and drawing lines
across our middles.
There is a windstorm
that swirls in there,
and then a fraction of a kite.
But you are lucky and safe
in there. You are wise too.
And you are throwing
Chakra bling into the sea.

One egg
undisturbed.
A bowl of milk.
There is a beautiful Mayan girl
holding you in her arms
underneath a full moon.
Feeling empty is elliptical
and we always come back
to the same place:
a vacant room or a galaxy
without stars and dust.
You say you are hungry,
and that there is nothing
left inside of you.
You are a stock car racing by
so fast it cannot be seen.

CHAPTER SIX

This is about Francesca Chabrier
This is about Hannah Brooks-Motl
This is about Emily Hunt
This is about Dara Wier
This is about Anne Holmes
This is about C. S. Ward
This is about Emily Toder
This is about Gale Thompson
This is about Ben Kopel
This is about Avi Kline
This is about Brian Foley
This is about Michele Christle
This is about Caroline Cabrera
This is about Homer, Max Jacob,
Nathaniel Hawthorne, John Cage,
Confucius, Marco Polo, this is about
Rimbaud, Pierre Reverdy, Marcel DuChamp,
Erik Satie, Jeffrey Dahmer,
German Children, this, Flying Object,
16 chances hanging on a line . . .

Please don't take it personally!

IN THE VALLEY ON A HILL

a Ferrari zooming
and agape
coming down
the big hill I live on
red and speedy
I wait for you
to invent a new gear
and ask Chelly
if who I want to be
is okay
because my brain is sharp
today and when it is
like this like a blade
I take my weaponry
into the tent I pitch
as high as the voice
I want to use
to sing to you all my friends
I know what people mean
when they say:
"I do not condone violence"
and hand you tiny deer
to put in your hair
but I'd like to crush you
nonetheless

LEAVE OF ABSENCE

It is raining in Texas, and we are all crying.
My mother calls. She is crying too.
She is tired of Texas. Texas is so tiring.
Texas is yawning. I can hear its mumbling
through the hole in my wall.
Texas come home.
Tell me what it feels like to come home.
Tell me how those sea legs feel.

COUNTDOWN TO SUMMER

I have a new body
can you hear the music
I am making
a glass violin
I I I I
feel young and old
at the same time
It is spring
the gray cat
is disappearing she is
a warm body of ash
I left my ring in your bed
and you are not my husband
and nothing is living
inside this new body
Look, the sky
is a close-up
of a man
in a perfect July
I say to him
just touch me
like a lake
like a lake
be a little confusing

THINGS OFTEN HAPPEN STRANGELY

When a faucet runs for too long
this is called overflow.
You must not drink from the overflow
because it is not reliable.
It does not behave properly
through a funnel, though it is
known to run to the brim of banks.
Regular water can be shut off.
You can take a bath in it,
or stick your head in the sink.
This feels good like descending
into a bed when you are so tired
that sleep is like an undetermined space.
But you must not be afraid of the overflow.
It is not like catching a bullet in your teeth,
or having a wolf at the door.
I am the mayor of this town,
and I can assure you that we will find a way
to keep the overflow from overflowing.
We've set up a fleet of beautiful boats
that can be converted into homes.
Each one has an eat in kitchen,
and an edible garden whcre you
can grow the most careful radishes.

PRETTY YOUNG THING

There is a falling piano.
It looks almost like
floating and full of glitter.
In my neighborhood
there is a girl.
I'd like to tell her
that when people go,
it is often for good like poof
and then absolutely nothing.
I want to practice how to love on her.
It's like the quilt, and the idea of the quilt.
I'd also like to say that I overdrew
from my bank account. It was
an uneasy combination
of a lump sum and her little wrists.

MILK BOTTLE POEM

white pool
you have no name
or lines
on your neck

smooth ounce of
zsa zsa

don't cry

and please
brush
your hair
and teeth
asap

CHAPTER SEVEN

THE BLIZZARD

There is a couch that keeps me
warm in the blizzard.
I fall asleep on it and wake up
in the middle of the night.
I often wonder how much time I waste
looking through old photographs.
There is one of me
on the beach in a polka dot bikini.
I am the lovechild
of the chief lifeguard and my mother.

There is a plane flying overhead.
I look up and say
Come on, just be smooth with it.
I imagine the pilot looking at me
with my favorite jacket on.
The bottom opens up
and lets a box drop.
It looks like a woman.
I wait for her to fall, so I can see
what kind of shape she makes in the snow.

There is no big splash.
The ice is like the slippery eye
of a whale. I cut down a tree,
you cut down a tree, the hunter
lets his gun fall while maintaining
excellent posture.

There is a garden in my backyard
and it is covered in snow.
I go inside to put on a sweater.
A child comes indoors,
and we both feel equally chilly.
The snowflakes look like spokes,
and the girl, a bit like a bicycle.

There is me inside a cabinet.
My horoscope says: jurassic storm.
I realize you are growing eyes
and very long fingers.
The fishing village is covered in snow,
but I am determined to cast a straight line.
I want to find my hat and my coat.
I want to eat canned goods out of your hands.

There is a man.
I am the man.
I am shaving a block of ice
in the shape of a blimp.

EPILOGUE

LAY FALLEN

French men surrounded by French snow.
Drifts and wind, or vice versa.
The cold all over, even through the sides of things.
Frozen horses in standard formation.
Me shoveling in nothing but a towel.
You pushing plows out of heaven.

ACKNOWLEDGMENTS

I would like to thank the editors of the following journals and anthologies in which some of these poems originally appeared: *Sink Review, Action, Yes, Jellyfish, Wolf in a Field, For Penelope, GlitterPony, Forklift, Ohio, Invisible Ear, Disco Prairie, Sixth Finch,* and *notnostrums.* Thank you also to Pilot Books for printing the chapbook *The Axioms.*

Thank you endlessly to: Wilfred Chabrier, Diana Chabrier, Julia Chabrier, Gabriela Chabrier, Kristina Chabrier, Hannah Brooks-Motl, Michele Christle, Phil Coredlli, Stella Corso, Blaire Gherts, Peter Gizzi, James Haug, Caroline Helfman, Emily Hunt, Emily Pettit, Guy Pettit, Alex Phillips, Amelia Sabetti, Caroline Sabetti, Sampson, Starkweather, Janaka Stucky, Paige Taggart, Emily Toder, Jono Tosch, Dylan Walker, Dara Wier, and Stefanie Zaitz for all of their love and support.

Special thanks goes to Sarah Gorham, Kristen Radtke, Kirby Gann, and the rest of the Sarabande family for their time, attention, and enthusiasm for my work.

FRANCESCA CHABRIER is the author of the chapbook *The Axioms* (Pilot Books, 2013). Her poems have appeared in *Action Yes, jubilat, notnostrums, Sixth Finch,* and *Sink Review,* among other journals. She is a graduate of the MFA Program for Poets and Writers at the University of Massachusetts at Amherst, and lives and writes in Oregon.

Sarabande Books thanks you for the purchase of this book; we do hope you enjoy it! Founded in 1994 as an independent, nonprofit, literary press, Sarabande publishes poetry, short fiction, and literary nonfiction—genres increasingly neglected by commercial publishers. We are committed to producing beautiful, lasting editions that honor exceptional writing, and to keeping those books in print. If you're interested in further reading, take a moment to browse our website, www. sarabandebooks.org. There you'll find information about other titles; opportunities to contribute to the Sarabande mission; and an abundance of supporting materials including audio, video, a lively blog, and our Sarabande in Education program.